In My Headspace: Reflective Poetry

Zuelene Troutt

Presentation by *BookLeaf Publishing*

Web: www.bookleafpub.com

E-mail: info@bookleafpub.com

ISBN: 9789363310889

First edition 2024

To my son, Lawson, - I hope you continue to love like no other, to hold on to that old soul of yours, and show the world what genuine love, kindness, and acceptance look like. I hope you continue to shine your light on others and make a difference in the world.

To the strongest women I know, my mom, Guada, and my sister, Lupe – you both have shown me time and time again what it means to overcome obstacles. You have no idea how much your words of encouragement have meant to me, and I will forever be grateful to have such amazing women to look up to.

ACKNOWLEDGEMENT

I will forever appreciate the unconditional love and support my family has given me. They've not only loved me through my successes but have loved me even more through my faults. I cannot repay you or credit you enough for showing me the true meaning of "unconditional" love. The same goes for the friends who have taken care of me emotionally, especially within the past three years. Hannah, Heather, Kimberly, Jessica, and Janina, thank you for the endless support you've given me without judgment.

PREFACE

Welcome to In My Headspace: Reflective Poetry. Here, you'll experience the full spectrum of my emotions and thoughts, from the exhilarating highs to the introspective lows. Each poem offers a glimpse into my inner world, capturing brief moments of clarity, struggle, and revelation. As you explore these verses, you'll see the world through my shifting perspective and emotions, giving you the opportunity to reflect on your own experiences and feelings.

The Journey

The past few chapters
were one and the same.
I kept hoping for more,
but I am to blame
for focusing on the
seemingly endless void,
and in the end,
became the one
who got destroyed.

My most recent chapter
was the worst of all.
I created a path
that would be my downfall.
I hid from the world,
my mistakes, and my shame
while still trying to hold on to
what could help keep me sane.

I can't keep this up,
and clinging to my past.
It feels like grasping at shadows,
slipping through my grasp.
It's time to let go,
to embrace what's ahead,

and rewrite the narrative,
that had filled me with dread.

Anxiety

3

I feel you
Grabbing hold of me,
Grasping my
intrusive thoughts,
Obsessing over
what I cannot control,
Seizing every form
of negativity,
and Capturing
every dark thought.
How do I let you go?

Facade

What you see
is what you don't get.
I lose myself
adapting to those around me.
I say what I need to,
so I can appease everyone.
I lose myself
conforming to the norms,
always afraid to speak my mind,
and risk letting others down.
I lose myself
ensuring everyone is happy
all the while, forgetting to love myself.

Invisible Battles

Don't cry.
Don't let them see you weak.
Don't let them see the storm brewing
underneath.

How do you do that?
How do you tell your mind, body, and soul
to simply let the past and everything else go?

Don't cry.
Don't make them shake you.
Don't let them in and constantly break you.

How do you do that?
How do you silence the ache,
And find the strength to finally awake?

When the Spark F A D E S

I once had
fire in my eyes,
knowing I had
insurmountable potential
in a world
filled with
a plethora of
possibilities.
You saw that fire,
you saw that potential,
and you loved me.

Now that the fire is out,
and all that is left
is a void,
a vast space
of untouched ambition,
and you see
the nothingness
that has swallowed me whole,
will you still love me?
Can you really say
that you will love me
through it all?

P a i n

You left me in a state of deep distress.
You left me with no chance to progress.
You shattered my spirit and my soul.
You made me feel lost in a chaotic mess.

You made me want to fade away.
And never see the light of day.
I lost myself in loving you.
While trying to pray the pain away.

I'm broken into a million pieces,
In a world where hope barely increases.
But pain is a cycle, endlessly turning,
Trying to heal where the hurt never ceases.

NEVER AGAIN

I once played the fool.
I once was so blind.
I once refused to see reality.
But N E V E R A G A I N.

I once folded within myself.
I once kept having intrusive thoughts.
I once wished I no longer existed.
But N E V E R A G A I N.

I once fed into your lies.
I once fed into your manipulation.
I once refused to stop loving you.
But N E V E R A G A I N.

S h a d o w s and R e g r e t

9

I broke my own heart today.
I killed my spirit and lost my way.
I fed my mind with lies and deceit.
I destroyed my soul and am now incomplete.

I can't seem to climb out of this hole I'm in.
My strength is gone, and my hope is thin.
How do I move forward and try to forget,
While seeking the light through shadows and
regret?

Cast Away

I try to cast away my worries
to remind myself that I am more
than the negative thoughts that consume me
and the feelings of worthlessness I can't ignore.

I try to cast away my shameful actions
that fight to kill my pride
and remind myself that I am only human
and let go of the disgrace I feel inside.

I try to cast away the endless stress
that life's trials can create,
to find calm within the chaos
and nurture a quiet state.

Seeking Solitude

Seeking solitude
in my isolation,
away from others' opinions
and manipulation.

Seeking solitude
from my faults,
to gain perspective
and untangle the knots.

Seeking solitude
to recalibrate my mind,
to soothe my restless spirit
and leave regret behind.

O n e D a y

One day, I will let this go.
Even though it hurts to know
That your heart was never mine.

One day, I will be okay.
I will be thankful along the way
To realize that I still have time.

One day, I will be stronger.
I will not have to wait any longer
For someone better to come my way.

One day, I will learn what love really is,
And cherish the moments I have missed,
And find the strength to see each day.

Living through Words

The stories I have read
have been my only escape
where I have lived vicariously
and experienced life through every page.

You see, I cannot travel where I wish to roam,
nor can I become who I long to be,
but through the countless characters,
I have found a way to stay free.

The stories I have read
helped me escape my intrusive thoughts.
They have been a refuge from every storm,
offering peace in every plot.

I have gained various forms of wisdom,
as well as strength and tranquility,
through the immense emotions
that have shaped and guided me.

Looking for Happiness

I looked for you in others,
in the posts, and all the likes.
I looked for you in their opinions,
and each time they told me I was right.

I looked for you in their approvals
and in every single embrace.
I looked for you in their solutions
for all the problems I faced.

I looked for you in my dreams,
in my wishes, wants, and needs.
I looked for you in every desire
and every ambition to succeed.

I looked for you with every fiber
in my unwavering soul.
I never wanted to lose you.
I never wanted to let you go.

I knew it was up to me
to keep choosing you.
But I felt so many moments
of losing you.

I got wrapped up in my selfishness
and need for more.
That I started losing sight of you
slipping away, unseen and unsure.

I finally realize now
that I've got to end my search.
I have to create you for myself
to match my spirit's worth.

Permission to Change

If you have been allowed to change
within the past few years,
then wouldn't I be allowed to change
and overcome my fears?

And if you were allowed to get knocked down
but get back up time and time again,
then wouldn't I be allowed to pick myself up
and find the strength to start again?

My trials and tribulations
may not be as great as yours,
but I'm allowed to overcome
the problems I couldn't face before.

I may not bear the type of trauma
that you have had to face,
but I'm still allowed to forgive and forget
the past I cannot erase.

Turning the Tide

Count me out
of the toxic environment you're living in.
I lived there once.
I won't live there again.

You thrived on the thought
of bringing me down,
of breaking my spirit,
and watching me drown.

You looked for the worst
in my presence alone
while I discovered solace,
in paths of my own.

Count me out of your life
and watch me succeed.
I'll rise above the noise,
and plant my own seed.

Unyielding Spirit

I woke up today feeling strong
for the first time in a while.
I know the worst has yet to come,
but I will embrace each and every trial.

Despite the obstacles I have already faced,
I have already come so far.
I've forgotten to count the blessings
that weave into my heart's memoir.

So here I am finally waking up
striving onward and ready to thrive,
knowing I have to keep moving forward,
fueled by resilience and a relentless drive.

Embracing Myself

o v e r a c h i e v e r
that's what I am called
for going above and beyond

u p t i g h t
that's what I am called
for the seriousness I exude

p e r f e c t i o n i s t
that's what I am called
for wanting to maintain control

I am M O R E
than what I am called by others

I am
p a s s i o n a t e
d e d i c a t e d
m o t i v a t e d
d i l i g e n t
g o a l - o r i e n t e d
f o c u s e d

and I refuse
to be ashamed

of all the
g r e a t things
I am called
to be.

Awakening P o t e n t i a l

One day, healing will start to flow,
and I will finally begin to know, saying,
"You are more than you see,
you are stronger, just be free."

One day, I'll smile with renewed light,
and feel that everything is alright, saying,
"You've conquered, you've achieved,
your heart is now relieved."

One day, strength will rise with grace,
and I will finally embrace this place, saying,
"You will open doors so wide,
you have God as your guide."

One day, I will see my worth unfold,
and with it, I will learn to be bold, saying,
"You will never be the same,
you will rise and own your name."

P o u r into M e

22

pour into me
lift me up
make me want to
live again
breathe again
wish again

pour into me
inspire me
make me want to
blossom again
grow again
thrive again

pour into me
elevate my spirit
make me want to
feel again
seek life and explore again
discover truth and live again

My F O R E V E R Kids

23

The light bulb moments,
the random messages
of past and present appreciation.

Those precious moments
that I did not think mattered at all
but actually mattered the most.

The updates of "This is how my child is doing,"
and the updates of "This is me,
and it was because of you."

The moments when I did not think
I would make a difference but
was reminded that I did in a way
I did not expect -
that had nothing to do with my career
and everything to do with my calling.

If you did not know how much
your voices and thoughts have affected me
in such a way that you became
a light in my life repeatedly,
you should know,
you are my "why," and

I cannot thank you enough for
making a difference in MY life.

(For my students in the past, present, and future)

Lawson

You are the
definition
of an "O l d S o u l."

You have this
ability to
r e a s o n
with situations
you shouldn't
u n d e r s t a n d
just yet.

I cannot
begin to fathom
your c a l l i n g,
your raison d'etre,
that G o d
has laid out for you.

Already,
at your youth,
Your kindness
Knows NO
b o u n d s,
and your light

Knows NO
f a d i n g.

May you
continue to
d e s i r e
to learn all
life has to offer
and
i n s p i r e
those around you.

You are my
l i g h t.
You are my
i n s p i r a t i o n.
You are my
reason for
b e i n g.

www.ingramcontent.com/pod-product-compliance
Lightning Source LLC
LaVergne TN
LVHW021331200726